INSPIRATIONS *of* LEADERSHIP

Quotes to Inspire the Leader in YOU!

Inspirations for Every Professional Woman...

BERNICE BOYDEN, SPHR, CEC

The Masterful Leader
Bernice@themasterfulleader.com
www.themasterfulleader.com

ISBN: 978-0-98269-912-6

NOTE FROM THE AUTHOR

Are you a good worker or a good leader? You were skilled in your job, and then you were p-r-o-m-o-t-e-d to a leadership role. Now what? Some people are promoted because they are a good worker, but no one ever gave them the tools to become a good leader. Well, this book will give you some leadership inspiration. Leadership is a difficult place to be, and the learning that comes along with the job never stops. I have compiled some very inspirational quotes that will force you to think about the leader that you are or the leader you would like to become.

With years of being a Human Resource Professional, I have counseled and coached hundreds of leaders and I have yet to meet one who doesn't want to be successful. This book is intended to be that daily nugget of inspiration when you feel you need a lift. Be inspired and keep up the good work!

ACKNOWLEDGEMENTS

With love, I dedicate this book to my loving family. My mom and dad because they've always believed in me and told me I could do whatever my heart desired. My husband, Alex, and children, Alexis and Alex… You are my inspiration. Thank you for believing in my big dreams and going on this journey with me! It's not over, hold on tight!

THANK YOU

Thank you to all of the leaders who allowed me to coach and counsel you to be the best you could be. I believed in each one of you, sometimes when you didn't believe in yourself. Again, thank you and I truly honor your effort; you have one of the hardest jobs ever!

LEADERSHIP

"Leadership is action, not position."
~Donald H. McGannon

My Thought:

Leadership is not an assignment;
it's a state of being…

Action Step:

What does leadership mean to you?

"The leadership instinct you
are born with is the backbone.
You develop the funny bone and
the wishbone that go with it."
~Elaine Agather

My Thought:
You can't stand without a backbone...

Action Step:
Is leadership in your bones?

"You can't lead anyone else further than you have gone yourself."
~Gene Mauch

My Thought:

Your mind can take you anywhere you want to go…

Action Step:

Where have you gone so far?

"Leaders are visionaries with a poorly developed sense of fear and no concept of the odds against them."
~Robert Jarvik

My Thought:
Ahh… FEAR, that four-letter word…

Action Step:
Are you leading through fear?
Or do you have no concept of the odds?

_____

_____

_____

_____

_____

_____

_____

_____

_____

"A leader is a dealer in hope."
~Napoleon Bonaparte, attributed

My Thought:

Hope is what everyone is thirsty for…

Action Step:

Look at your leadership style.
What are you a dealer of?

"Leaders don't create followers,
they create more leaders."
~Tom Peters

My Thought:
Mentor someone. You won't live forever…

Action Step:
What type of people are you creating?

"A good leader is a person who takes a little more than his share of the blame and a little less than his share of the credit."
~John C. Maxwell

My Thought:

A true leader takes his/her losses, and doesn't boast…

Action Step:

Do you blame or take all the credit?

"The real leader has no need to lead—
he is content to point the way."
~Henry Miller

My Thought:

A true leader does not need the entire spotlight…

Action Step:

What do you need, as a leader?

"I suppose that leadership at one time meant muscle, but today it means getting along with people."
~Indira Gandhi

My Thought:
Leadership has nothing to do with your physical muscle; and everything to do with your mental muscle…

Action Step:
What muscle do you use in your leadership?

"*The best executive is the one who has sense enough to pick good men to do what he wants done, and self-restraint enough to keep from meddling with them while they do it.*"
~Theodore Roosevelt

My Thought:
Leadership begins with trust…

Action Step:
Are you trusting or meddling?

*"Leadership is based on a spiritual quality;
the power to inspire, the power to
inspire others to follow."*
~Vince Lombardi

My Thought:
Leaders inspire the heart…

Action Step:
What powers do you possess as a leader?

"We have great managers who haven't spent a day in management school. Do we have great surgeons that haven't spent a day in surgical school?"
~Henry Mintzberg

My Thought:

Leadership doesn't always have to be learned…

Action Step:

What innate leadership skills do you have?

_____

_____

_____

_____

_____

_____

_____

_____

_____

*"The art of leadership is saying no, not yes.
It is very easy to say yes."*
~Tony Blair

My Thought:

It takes guts to say no...

Action Step:

What's your answer: Yes or No?

"*Management is nothing more
than motivating other people.*"
~Lee Iacocca

My Thought:
Motivation is a top priority for leaders…

Action Step:
Are you motivating?

*"A leader has the vision and conviction
that a dream can be achieved. He inspires
the power and energy to get it done."*
~Ralph Nader

My Thought:

Inspiring the hope is a leader's role…

Action Step:

What do you inspire as a leader?

*"If your actions inspire others to dream more,
learn more, do more and become more,
you are a leader."*
~ John Quincy Adams

My Thought:

It's true that your action inspires others…

Action Step:

What actions are you putting forth?

_____

_____

_____

_____

_____

_____

_____

_____

_____

_____

ENCOURAGEMENT

*"When you come to the end of your rope,
tie a knot and hang on."*
~Franklin D. Roosevelt

My Thought:
Never let go of the rope…

Action Step:
Do you hold on or let go when you
reach the end of your rope?

"One of the most beautiful gifts in the world is the gift of encouragement. When someone encourages you, that person helps you over a threshold you might otherwise never have crossed on your own."
~John O'Donohue

My Thought:

It takes a big heart to encourage others...

Action Step:

Do you have an encouraging heart?

*"Never give in... never, never, never, never,
in nothing great or small, large or petty, never
give in except to convictions of honor and good
sense. Never yield to force... never yield to the
apparently overwhelming might of the enemy."*
~Winston Churchill

My Thought:

Giving in easily doesn't work with the enemy…

Action Step:

When do you give in?

"Go over, go under, go around or go through.
But never give up."
~Unknown

My Thought:

This is so true; never give up…

Action Step:

Do you do all of these steps before you give up?

"Instead of giving myself reasons why I can't,
I give myself reasons why I can."
~Unknown

My Thought:

Doubt can tell you all of the reasons that you
can't…

Action Step:

Do you listen to why you can't,
or believe that you can?

"Risk more than others think is safe.
Care more than others think is wise.
Dream more than others think is practical.
Expect more than others think is possible."
~Claude Bissell

My Thought:
Jump off the edge…

Action Step:
Do you challenge yourself to jump off the edge?

*"A diamond is merely a lump of coal
that did well under pressure."*
~Unknown

My Thought:

Wow! Pressure creates great things…

Action Step:

What do you become under pressure?

"Trust yourself.
You know more than you think you do."
~Benjamin Spock

My Thought:
Trust yourself…

Action Step:
Do you believe in yourself enough
to trust yourself?

SUCCESS

*"Try not to become a man of success,
but rather try to become a man of value."*
~Albert Einstein

My Thought:
Value beats success any day of the week…

Action Step:
Are you a man/woman of success and value?
Can you have one without the other?

"Success without honor is an unseasoned dish;
it will satisfy your hunger,
but it won't taste good."
~Joe Paterno

My Thought:
Honor is one of the keys to success…

Action Step:
Where is your honor?

*"I couldn't wait for success...
so I went ahead without it."*
~Jonathan Winters

My Thought:
Success is…

Action Step:
Did you go ahead or are you waiting?

"Don't aim for success if you want it;
just do what you love and believe in it,
and it will come naturally."
~David Frost

My Thought:

Doing what you love is one meaning of success…

Action Step:

What are you really aiming for?

_____
_____
_____
_____
_____
_____
_____
_____
_____
_____

"Judge your success by what you had to give up in order to get it."
~Unknown

My Thought:

Success sometimes comes with sacrifice…

Action Step:

What did you give up to get success?
What have you given up so far?

"The difference between a successful person and others is not a lack of strength, not a lack of knowledge, but rather a lack of will."
~Vince Lombardi

My Thought:
Can you have success without will?

Action Step:
Do you have the will to succeed?

"Success is blocked by concentrating on it and planning for it... Success is shy—it won't come out while you're watching."
~Tennessee Williams

My Thought:
A watched pot never boils…

Action Step:
What are you watching or over-focusing on?

"*Success is to be measured not so much by the position that one has reached in life as by the obstacles which he has overcome.*"
~Booker T. Washington

My Thought:
Success means so much more when earned…

Action Step:
How do you measure success?

"Sometimes it is better to lose and do the right thing than to win and do the wrong thing."
~Tony Blair

My Thought:
Winning is not the end all be all…

Action Step:
Is winning everything to you?

"To lead people, walk beside them....
As for the best leaders, the people do not
notice their existence. The next best,
the people honor and praise. The next,
the people fear; and the next, the people hate....
When the best leader's work is done the
people say, 'We did it ourselves!'"
~Lao-tsu

My Thought:
Leadership is not always about
standing out front…

Action Step:
Do you have to always be out front?

*"Control is not leadership; management
is not leadership; leadership is leadership.
If you seek to lead, invest at least 50% of your time
in leading yourself – your own purpose, ethics,
principles, motivation, conduct.
Invest at least 20% leading those with authority
over you and 15% leading your peers."*
~Dee Hock,
Founder and CEO Emeritus, Visa

My Thought:
Look inward for the leadership…

Action Step:
What percentages do you spend on yourself
and others?

"*All of the great leaders have had one characteristic in common: It was the willingness to confront unequivocally the major anxiety of their people in their time. This, and not much else, is the essence of leadership.*"
~John Kenneth Galbraith

My Thought:
Comfort for confrontation is key in leadership…

Action Step:
Are you comfortable confronting?

"The task of the leader is to get his people from where they are to where they have not been."
~Henry Kissinger

My Thought:
Easier to push than to pull…

Action Step:
Are you pushing or pulling?

"Never give an order that can't be obeyed."
~General Douglas MacArthur

My Thought:

Always be willing to take a dose of your
own medicine…

Action Step:

Can you obey all of your orders/advice?

*"Great leaders are almost always great simplifiers,
who can cut through argument, debate, and
doubt to offer a solution
everybody can understand."*
~General Colin Powell

My Thought:
Put in layman terms…

Action Step:
Are you a simplifier or complicator?

"Leadership is intentional influence."
~Michael McKinney

My Thought:

Influence is the magic of leadership…

Action Step:

What's your influence level?
What are you doing to gain or get greater
influence?

_____

_____

_____

_____

_____

_____

_____

TESTIMONIALS

"Bernice is a polished business professional and a great personal coach. She brings a host of wonderful leadership and human relations expertise into her profession, and uniquely blends her strong organizational and technical skills with an inspired business savvy."

—M. SPILMAN

"As a Senior Manager who has worked with her for several years, I find her strong skills to be in the areas of coaching, intellect, and leadership. Intellect: Bernice quickly understands the issue you're dealing with and offers excellent solutions. Coaching: She learns the people involved and offers excellent coaching guidance. Leadership: Bernice has excellent decision-making skills, supports her position with logic and facts, and always remains calm and professional. She is confidential and trustworthy in all matters. Bernice is confident yet remains humble. She's about helping the people she supports and never about promoting herself – which I really respect."

— J. PELUSO

Bernice Boyden, SPHR, CEC

Leadership Development Expert, Bernice Boyden, is fiercely committed to showing women in leadership on how to unleash their influence, gain more respect, confidence and be the "go-to" leader in the workplace. When you apply her "IT" Factor techniques, you will gain fast results at work and in your personal life. Guiding you to achieve the ultimate success as a leader with time tested, proven, and easy to learn tips—without you losing your sanity—is her passion and commitment. Bernice offers her no-nonsense, truth-telling, personal transparency and open communication style with all of her clients. Using her "best-friend" charisma, clients often feel like they've known Bernice all of their lives. For almost two decades while working as a Human Resources professional in several large Fortune 50 companies, Bernice had coached many elite-level leaders, implementing one-of-a-kind techniques that unleash strengths, maximize influence, increase respect and produce immediate results. Bernice is the author of two books, *Inspirations to Leadership-Words of Wisdom for the Leader in You* and *Seven Success Secrets for Every Woman in Leadership*.

Visit Bernice at www.themasterfulleader.com.

ALSO BY BERNICE BOYDEN

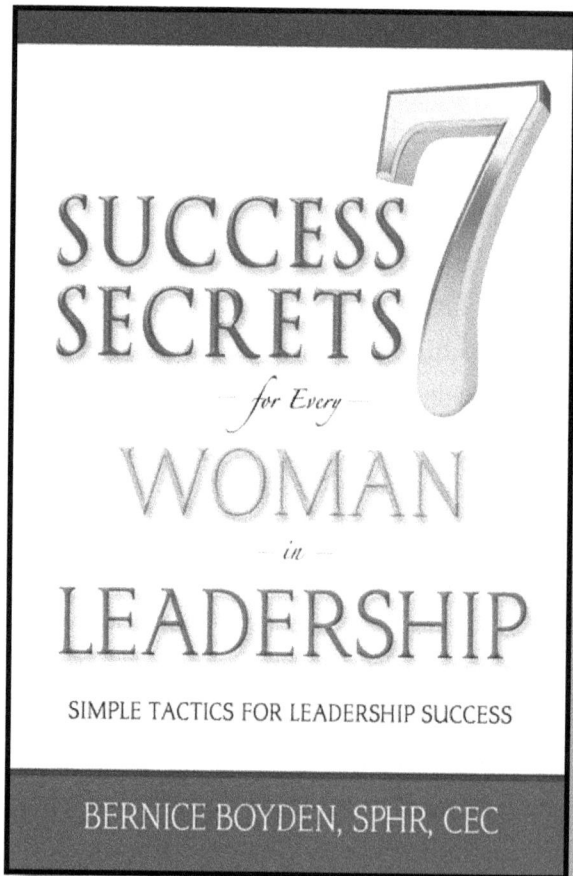

SUCCESS SECRETS 7

for Every

WOMAN

in

LEADERSHIP

SIMPLE TACTICS FOR LEADERSHIP SUCCESS

BERNICE BOYDEN, SPHR, CEC

www.ingramcontent.com/pod-product-compliance
Lightning Source LLC
Chambersburg PA
CBHW071336200326
41520CB00013B/3004